MY FIVE SENSES

Sight

Published by Smart Apple Media, 1980 Lookout Drive, North Mankato, Minnesota 56003.
Printed in the United States of America

PHOTOGRAPHS BY Richard Cummins, Tom Myers, Photo Researchers, Inc. (John Daugherty), Bonnie Sue Rauch, Tom Stack & Associates
(Thomas Kitchin, J. Lotter), Unicorn Stock Photos (Eric R. Berndt, Ed Harp, Gary Randall, Dennis Thompson)
DESIGN Evansday Design

Library of Congress Cataloging-in-Publication Data
Hidalgo, Maria.
Sight / by Maria Hidalgo.
p. cm. — (My five senses)
Summary: Briefly describes the parts of the eye and how it enables us to see.
Includes bibliographical references and index.
ISBN 1-58340-303-5
1. Vision—Juvenile literature. [1. Vision. 2. Eye. 3. Senses and sensation.] I. Title. II. My five senses (North Mankato, Minn.)
QP475.7 .H515 2003
612.84—dc21   2002030908
First Edition
2 4 6 8 9 7 5 3 1

MY FIVE SENSES

Sight

MARIA HIDALGO

4

YOUR SENSES HELP YOU LEARN

5

ABOUT THE WORLD AROUND YOU.

There are 5 senses:

TASTE

TOUCH

SMELL

HEARING

SIGHT.

Your eyes give you your sense of sight.

Your eyes help you see danger,
so you can stay safe.

You see people you love.

You see things that make you
cry or laugh.

You see words to read
and balls to catch.

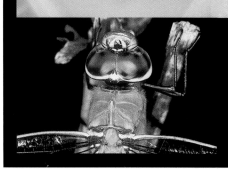

A dragonfly's eyes are so big that they
take up most of its head.

Your eyes can do many things.

They can see colors.

They can see in

BRIGHT LIGHT
AND DARK ROOMS.

They can even tell you how far
away something is.

An eagle can see a mouse on the ground
from one mile (1.6 km) away.

8

EYES COME IN MANY

DIFFERENT COLORS.

Some people have

BROWN EYES.

Others have

BLUE

OR GREEN EYES.

But all eyes work the same way.

You cannot see without light.

The **pupil** in your eye lets light in.

Your eye sees colors and shapes.

And it sees them upside-down!

The colored part of your eye is called the iris. No two irises look exactly the same.

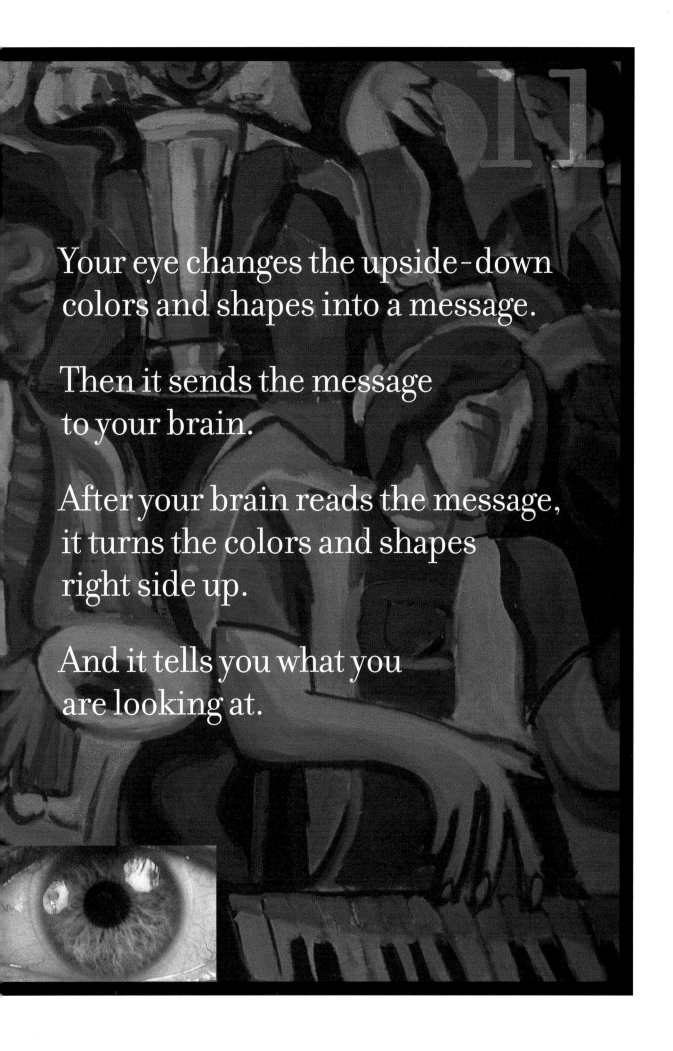

Your eye changes the upside-down
colors and shapes into a message.

Then it sends the message
to your brain.

After your brain reads the message,
it turns the colors and shapes
right side up.

And it tells you what you
are looking at.

12

EYES CAN BE EASILY HURT, SO

THEY NEED TO BE **PROTECTED.**

Your body protects your eyes with

EYELIDS,
EYELASHES,
AND TEARS.

Your eyelid works like a
windshield wiper on a car.

Every time you blink,
dirt is pushed off your eye.

Your eyelid also keeps things
from poking your eye.

If something gets too close
to your eye, you blink.

People have round pupils. But some animals
have pupils shaped like lines or rectangles.

Your eyelashes are like curtains.

They help block bright light.

And they catch dirt before it
gets into your eye.

If dirt does get into your eye,
tears wash it away.

Tears clean your eyes
and keep them moist.

16

SOME PEOPLE CANNOT SEE WELL.

THEY WEAR GLASSES TO SEE BETTER.

Blind people cannot see at all.

They use their other
senses to do things.

Blind people may listen for cars
before crossing a street.

They may use their sense
of touch to read **Braille**.

Seeing Eye dogs are dogs that are trained to help blind people.

They help them cross the street and climb stairs.

They help them find things.

And they help keep them safe.

German shepherds, Doberman pinschers, and retrievers are the most popular kinds of Seeing Eye dogs.

It is important to take
care of your eyes.

Do not look into bright lights.

Never look at the sun.

And do not poke your eyes or rub
them too hard.

There is so much in the world
to look at!

Each letter and number in Braille
is made of one to six raised dots, or bumps.

20

Braille an alphabet of raised dots that blind people can read with their fingers

protected kept safe

pupil the round, black opening in the middle of your eye

senses things that let you see, smell, taste, hear, and touch the world around you

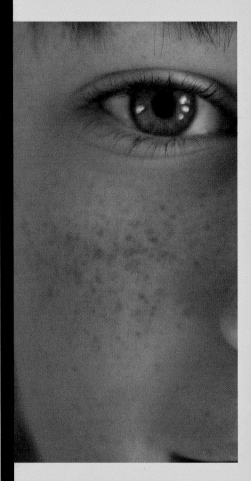

Big Pupils, Little Pupils

Your pupils are different sizes in the light and in the dark. This activity will show you how quickly they can change size.

WHAT YOU NEED

A dark closet

A sunny day

A friend

WHAT YOU DO

1. Have your friend sit in the closet with her eyes closed. Count to 100.

2. Now, with your friend's eyes still closed, lead her outside.

3. On the count of three, have her open her eyes.

4. What size are her pupils at first? What size do they become? Do they change quickly or slowly? Did your friend feel anything when she opened her eyes?

Read More

Cole, Joanna. *Magic School Bus Explores the Senses*.
New York: Scholastic, 2001.

Hurwitz, Sue. *Sight*. Danbury, Conn.: Franklin Watts, 1999.

Molter, Carey. *Sense of Sight*. Edina, Minn.:
Abdo Publishing Company, 2002.

Explore the Web

KIDSHEALTH

http://kidshealth.org/kid

NEUROSCIENCE FOR KIDS: THE SENSES

http://faculty.washington.edu/chudler/chsense.html

THINKQUEST: COME TO YOUR SENSES

http://tqjunior.thinkquest.org/3750